# A Prima Facie Case
## Your 14th Psychiatric Consultation
## William Yee M.D., J.D.
## Copyright Applied for 07/03/2020

A prima facie case involves a complaint with all of the elements necessary to support a judgment and sufficient to defeat a motion for summary judgment to dismiss for failure to make a claim.

This is an introduction from the point of view of psychiatrists, mental health providers, administrators, city, county, and state agencies at risk for medical malpractice lawsuits.

The reader is advised to consult with a practicing attorney in his place of practice for legal advice and legal representation.

This missive is simply an introduction to give the reader the vocabulary necessary to carry a rational conversation with the licensed attorney.

My advice is merely to read this to assist you in your communication with a practicing attorney who will give you legal advice.

The psychiatrist, nurse practitioner, nurse, psychologist, social worker and psychiatric technician at the point of service are entangled by the contract to provide health care services according to their level of training and experience.

The contract is created when the patient asks for health care and the health care provider agrees to provide the health care.

The first question you ask the attorney is, "am I in a contractual relationship that allows this person to sue me for this act on my part?"

An injury from the health care service may give rise to a lawsuit if the injury is an injury that the patient did not accept as a potential outcome from the treatment.

The second question that you ask is, "was there an injury from my interaction with the patient?"

The injury may have been caused by another actor than yourself.

Was the patient informed of the risk of the specific injury alleged?

That situation arises when the patient is not informed of that possible injury as a complication of the treatment offered.

The third question you ask, "is there informed consent such that although the injury happened, it was a risk that the patient accepted prior to my treatment?"

At this point the attorney might advise you that, "if it wasn't in writing, it didn't happen."

That is why the patient is asked to sign informed consent forms.

That is why advertising on television gives a long list of complications during the advertising.

That is why the pharmacist gives the patient a "package insert" with a list of benefits and risks along with the medications.

That is why the healthcare provider educates the patient as to the risks involved and has the patient sign a consent to treatment form.

After informed consent is perfected a lawsuit may result if neglect, incompetence, or other breach of contract violates the best practice at the time of service according to the level of training, experience and licensing of the healthcare provider.

For example, being reckless in prescribing large doses of medication.

Reckless means that the prescriber knew or should have known that the dose was larger than peers would prescribe under the same circumstances.

Another example would be intoxication resulting in poor surgical technique and injury.

That is why the medical records are so thick.

Every possible detail is documented.

That documentation is done at the time of the service or shortly after the service.

The medical record made at or about the time of the service is in fact admissible as evidence as an exception to the hearsay rule.

The hearsay rule states that out of court statements cannot be admitted into evidence unless there is a specific exception.

A medical record is made out of court and therefore would be inadmissible.

However, because it is a Present Sense Impression stated at or about the time the witness perceived the event, it is admissible as evidence.

This is very important, because it allows the medical record to be admitted by the nurse, the social worker, the psychologist, the administrator, the city, the county, and the state agencies and personnel who may not have been present at the time of service, but may be accountable by virtue of many legal concepts.

The fourth question you ask, "is there negligence on my part sufficient to support a judgment against me?"

At this point your attorney will want to review the record or have it reviewed by an expert to determine if your care met the standard of care practiced by others with your training and experience at that time and place.

Respondeat Superior allows the plaintiff attorney to name the chain of command above the healthcare provider as defendants for a variety of reasons.

The chain of command makes policy, procedure, and practice that the healthcare providers are required to comply with.

The chain of command provides the health care records.

The chain of command provides staffing during clinic hours, evenings, weekends and holidays.

If the staffing is not adequate, then care cannot be provided, or it is provided and documented poorly due to lack of time and lack of resources.

If you are in the chain of command the fifth question you ask is, "am I involved sufficiently as an administrator to support a judgment against me on the basis of Respondeat Superior?"

Your attorney will want to look at the policies, procedures and practices of your agency. He will want records of committee meetings that connect you to the service provider.

Here, there is no leash on the billable hours. Very often the billable hours could bankrupt an agency. Many claims are settled out of court to avoid the legal costs.

If you are an administrator in a state agency your actions may fall under statutory immunities.

Each state has constitutional or statutory immunities. In California you should review the following and then ask your attorney how the following applies to you and the facts that potentially give rise to a cause of action against you and your assets:

ARTICLE 2. Liability of Public Entities [815 - 818.9] ( Article 2 added by Stats. 1963, Ch. 1681.)
815.1
 Except as otherwise provided by statute:
(a) A public entity is not liable for an injury, whether such injury arises out of an act or omission of the public entity or a public employee or any other person.
(b) The liability of a public entity established by this part (commencing with Section 814) is subject to any immunity of the public entity provided by statute, including this part, and is subject to any defenses that would be available to the public entity if it were a private person.

(Added by Stats. 1963, Ch. 1681.)
815.2

(a) A public entity is liable for injury proximately caused by an act or omission of an employee of the public entity within the scope of his employment if the act or omission would, apart from this section, have given rise to a cause of action against that employee or his personal representative.

(b) Except as otherwise provided by statute, a public entity is not liable for an injury resulting from an act or omission of an employee of the public entity where the employee is immune from liability.
(Added by Stats. 1963, Ch. 1681.)
815.3.

(a) Notwithstanding any other provision of this part, unless the elected official and the public entity are named as codefendants in the same action, a public entity is not liable to a plaintiff under this part for any act or omission of an elected official employed by or otherwise representing that public entity, which act or omission constitutes an intentional tort, including, but not limited to, harassment, sexual battery, and intentional infliction of emotional distress. For purposes of this section, harassment in violation of state or federal law constitutes an intentional tort, to the extent permitted by federal law. This section shall not apply to defamation.

(b) If the elected official is held liable for an intentional tort other than defamation in such an action, the trier of fact in reaching the verdict shall determine if the act or omission constituting the intentional tort arose from and was directly related to the elected official's performance of his or her official duties. If the trier of fact determines that the act or omission arose from and was directly related to the elected official's performance of his or her official duties, the public entity shall be liable for the judgment as provided by law. For the purpose of this subdivision, employee managerial functions shall be deemed to arise from, and to directly relate to, the elected official's official duties. However, acts or omissions constituting sexual harassment shall not be deemed to arise from, and to directly relate to, the elected official's official duties.

(c) If the trier of fact determines that the elected official's act or omission did not arise from and was not directly related to the elected official's performance of his or her official duties, upon a final judgment, including any appeal, the plaintiff shall first seek recovery of the judgment against the assets of the elected official. If the court determines that the elected official's assets are insufficient to satisfy the total judgment, including plaintiff's costs as provided by law, the court shall determine the amount of the deficiency and the plaintiff may seek to collect that remainder of the judgment from the public entity. The public entity may pay that deficiency if the public entity is otherwise authorized by law to pay that judgment.

(d) To the extent the public entity pays any portion of the judgment against the elected official pursuant to subdivision (c) or has expended defense costs in an action in which the trier of fact determines the elected official's action did not arise from and did not directly relate to his or her performance of official duties, the public entity shall pursue all available creditor's remedies against the elected official in indemnification, including garnishment, until the elected official has fully reimbursed the public entity.

(e) If the public entity elects to appeal the judgment in an action brought pursuant to this section, the entity shall continue to provide a defense for the official until the case is finally adjudicated, as provided by law.

(f) It is the intent of the Legislature that elected officials assume full fiscal responsibility for their conduct which constitutes an intentional tort not directly related to their official duties committed for which the public entity they represent may also be liable, while maintaining fair compensation for those persons injured by such conduct.

(g) This section shall not apply to a criminal or civil enforcement action brought on behalf of the state by an elected district attorney, city attorney, or Attorney General.

(h) If any provision of this section or the application thereof to any person or circumstances is held invalid, that invalidity shall not affect other provisions or applications of the section which can be given effect without the invalid provision or application, and to this end

the provisions of this section are severable.
(Added by Stats. 1994, Ch. 796, Sec. 1. Effective January 1, 1995.)
815.4.

A public entity is liable for injury proximately caused by a tortious act or omission of an independent contractor of the public entity to the same extent that the public entity would be subject to such liability if it were a private person. Nothing in this section subjects a public entity to liability for the act or omission of an independent contractor if the public entity would not have been liable for the injury had the act or omission been that of an employee of the public entity.
(Added by Stats. 1963, Ch. 1681.)
815.6.

Where a public entity is under a mandatory duty imposed by an enactment that is designed to protect against the risk of a particular kind of injury, the public entity is liable for an injury of that kind proximately caused by its failure to discharge the duty unless the public entity establishes that it exercised reasonable diligence to discharge the duty.

(Added by Stats. 1963, Ch. 1681.)
816.

A public entity is not liable for injury arising out of any activity conducted by a member of the California National Guard pursuant to Section 316, 502, 503, 504, or 505 of Title 32 of the United States Code and compensated pursuant to the Federal Tort Claims Act.

It is the intent of the Legislature, in enacting this section, to conform state law regarding liability for activities of the National Guard to federal law as expressed in Public Law 97-124.

(Added by Stats. 1982, Ch. 616, Sec. 1.)
818.

Notwithstanding any other provision of law, a public entity is not liable for damages awarded under Section 3294 of the Civil Code or other damages imposed primarily for the sake of example and by way of punishing the defendant.

(Added by Stats. 1963, Ch. 1681.)
818.2.

A public entity is not liable for an injury caused by adopting or failing to adopt an enactment or by failing to enforce any law.

(Added by Stats. 1963, Ch. 1681.)

818.4.

A public entity is not liable for an injury caused by the issuance, denial, suspension or revocation of, or by the failure or refusal to issue, deny, suspend or revoke, any permit, license, certificate, approval, order, or similar authorization where the public entity or an employee of the public entity is authorized by enactment to determine whether or not such authorization should be issued, denied, suspended or revoked.
(Added by Stats. 1963, Ch. 1681.)
818.5.

The Department of Motor Vehicles is liable for any injury to a lienholder or good faith purchaser of a vehicle proximately caused by the department's negligent omission of the lienholder's name from an ownership certificate issued by the department. The liability of the department under this section shall not exceed the actual cash value of the vehicle.
(Added by Stats. 1985, Ch. 437, Sec. 2.)
818.6.

A public entity is not liable for injury caused by its failure to make an inspection, or by reason of making an

inadequate or negligent inspection, of any property, other than its property (as defined in subdivision (c) of Section 830), for the purpose of determining whether the property complies with or violates any enactment or contains or constitutes a hazard to health or safety.
(Added by Stats. 1963, Ch. 1681.)
818.7.

No board, commission, or any public officer or employee of the state or of any district, county, city and county, or city is liable for any damage or injury to any person resulting from the publication of any reports, records, prints, or photographs of or concerning any person convicted of violation of any law relating to the use, sale, or possession of controlled substances, when such publication is to school authorities for use in instruction on the subject of controlled substances or to any person when used for the purpose of general education. However, the name of any person concerning whom any such reports, records, prints, or photographs are used shall be kept confidential and every reasonable effort shall be made to

maintain as confidential any information which may tend to identify such person.
(Amended by Stats. 1984, Ch. 1635, Sec. 40.)
818.8.

A public entity is not liable for an injury caused by misrepresentation by an employee of the public entity, whether or not such misrepresentation be negligent or intentional.
(Added by Stats. 1963, Ch. 1681.)
818.9.

A court or county, its employees, independent contractors, and volunteers shall not be liable because of any advice provided to small claims court litigants or potential litigants as a public service on behalf of the court or county pursuant to the Small Claims Act (Chapter 5.5 (commencing with Section 116.110) of Title 1 of Part 1 of the Code of Civil Procedure).
(Amended by Stats. 2002, Ch. 806, Sec. 24. Effective January 1, 2003.)

Having read the above if you are in the chain of command in a governmental agency the sixth question you ask is, "am I protected by governmental immunity or at risk?"

Your attorney will want to examine the policies, procedures and practices of your agency that impact the health care provider at the point of service.

Your attorney will want to examine your job description and your participation actions that impact the health care provider at the point of service.

Your attorney will want to see records of your participation in committee activities and other agency activities, official and unofficial.

If you are an administrator in a State Agency you may be, "acting under the color of state law." That means you are exercising the power of the state.

Review the following:
42 U.S. Code § 1983.Civil action for deprivation of rights
Every person who, under color of any statute, ordinance, regulation, custom, or usage, of any State or Territory or the

District of Columbia, subjects, or causes to be subjected, any citizen of the United States or other person within the jurisdiction thereof to the deprivation of any rights, privileges, or immunities secured by the Constitution and laws, shall be liable to the party injured in an action at law, suit in equity, or other proper proceeding for redress, except that in any action brought against a judicial officer for an act or omission taken in such officer's judicial capacity, injunctive relief shall not be granted unless a declaratory decree was violated or declaratory relief was unavailable.

For the purposes of this section, any Act of Congress applicable exclusively to the District of Columbia shall be considered to be a statute of the District of Columbia. (R.S. § 1979; Pub. L. 96–170, § 1, Dec. 29, 1979, 93 Stat. 1284; Pub. L. 104–317, title III, § 309(c), Oct. 19, 1996, 110 Stat. 3853.)

42 U.S. Code § 1985.Conspiracy to interfere with civil rights

(1) Preventing officer from performing duties

If two or more persons in any State or Territory conspire to prevent, by force, intimidation, or threat, any person from accepting or holding any office, trust, or place of confidence under the United States, or from discharging any duties thereof; or to induce by like means any officer of the United States to leave any State, district, or place, where his duties as an officer are required to be performed, or to injure him in his person or property on account of his lawful discharge of the duties of his office, or while engaged in the lawful discharge thereof, or to injure his property so as to molest, interrupt, hinder, or impede him in the discharge of his official duties;

(2)Obstructing justice; intimidating party, witness, or juror

If two or more persons in any State or Territory conspire to deter, by force, intimidation, or threat, any party or witness in any court of the United States from attending such court, or from testifying to any matter pending therein, freely, fully, and truthfully, or to injure such party or witness in his person or property on account of his having so attended or testified, or to influence the verdict, presentment, or indictment of any grand or petit juror in any such court, or to injure such juror in his person or property on account of any verdict, presentment, or indictment lawfully assented to by him, or of his being or having been such juror; or if two or more persons conspire for the purpose of impeding, hindering, obstructing, or defeating, in any manner, the due course of justice in any State or Territory, with intent to deny to any citizen the equal protection of the laws, or to injure him or his property for lawfully enforcing, or attempting to enforce, the right of any person, or class of persons, to the equal protection of the laws;

(3) Depriving persons of rights or privileges

If two or more persons in any State or Territory conspire or go in disguise on the highway or on the premises of another, for the purpose of depriving, either directly or indirectly, any person or class of persons of the equal protection of the laws, or of equal privileges and immunities under the laws; or for the purpose of preventing or hindering the constituted authorities of any State or Territory from giving or securing to all persons within such State or Territory the equal protection of the laws; or if two or

more persons conspire to prevent by force, intimidation, or threat, any citizen who is lawfully entitled to vote, from giving his support or advocacy in a legal manner, toward or in favor of the election of any lawfully qualified person as an elector for President or Vice President, or as a Member of Congress of the United States; or to injure any citizen in person or property on account of such support or advocacy; in any case of conspiracy set forth in this section, if one or more persons engaged therein do, or cause to be done, any act in furtherance of the object of such conspiracy, whereby another is injured in his person or property, or deprived of having and exercising any right or privilege of a citizen of the United States, the party so injured or deprived may have an action for the recovery of damages occasioned by such injury or deprivation, against any one or more of the conspirators.
(R.S. § 1980.)

Having read the above and if you are in the chain of command in a state governmental agency the seventh question you ask is, "was I acting under color of state law such that I am at risk?"

Again, your attorney will want to examine the policies, procedures and practices of your agency that impact the health care provider at the point of service.

Your attorney will want to examine your job description and your participation in actions that impact the health care provider at the point of service.

Your attorney will want to see records of your participation in committee activities and other agency activities official and unofficial.

If your agency is a state hospital or prison under an existing court order your actions may be in violation of that existing court order.

Governmental immunity was not established to permit state agencies and employees of state agencies to commit crimes, conspire to commit crimes, violate court orders, or to conspire to violate court orders.

The plaintiff attorney may have an opportunity to establish an exception to governmental immunity based upon violation of a court order.

The eighth question you ask, "was my conduct in violation of a court order such that the plaintiff may persuade the court to find an exception to governmental immunity?"

Your attorney will want to review the court order and your activities under the court order

During your initial visit with an attorney, you will ask about anticipated court costs and fees and you will negotiate a retainer and schedule of payments for his hourly wage.

That can be a painful experience that may be mitigated by malpractice insurance.

If your conduct was criminal conduct your malpractice insurance may not cover you.

If you fail to notify your malpractice insurance carrier promptly you may waive your claim to your malpractice insurance.

If you have malpractice insurance your ninth question is, "will my malpractice insurance pay for legal fees and a judgment?"

Generally, it is against the law for state agencies to pay for legal fees, court costs and judgments for criminal behaviors of its employees.

Your tenth question is, "will the state pay for legal fees, court costs and judgments if my conduct was criminal?"

If your conduct was not criminal your employer may or may not pay for legal fees and a judgment.

State agencies will usually pay for legal fees and a judgment if you were following policies, procedures and practices established by the agency.

Very often the agency will not pay legal fees, court costs and judgments if your conduct was in violation of policies, practices, and procedures.

Your eleventh question will be, "was my conduct in violation of policies, procedures and practices of the agency such that the agency will not pay court costs, legal fees and the judgment?"

Again, your attorney will want to examine the policies, procedures and practices of your agency that impact the health care provider at the point of service.

Your attorney will want to examine your job description and your participation actions that impact the health care provider at the point of service.

Your attorney will want to see records of your participation in committee activities and other agency activities official and unofficial.

You will have further discussion of your legal posture based upon your attorney's knowledge and experience in his state, the constitution of his state, the statutes of his state and the case law of his state.

Although I am licensed to practice law in Michigan, I have a very limited practice and even in Michigan I refer people to practicing attorneys as I practice psychiatry and my interface with the law is primarily as an expert witness in probate court and civil and criminal trials.

I have very limited experience as a trial attorney and no experience as a prosecuting attorney and no experience as a defense attorney.

I therefore do not give legal advice, except to recommend that you consult with a practicing attorney in your jurisdiction.

That said, I am going to examine situations that I think are likely to result in a summons, complaints, and judgments against practitioners in the future.

They include the practice of prescribing addicting medications, polypharmacy,

and treating developmentally disabled
dependent adults.

First, the long-term use of addicting
medication is generally contraindicated
for the mentally ill.
Benzodiazepines Tied to a 41% Increased
Mortality Risk in AD
Batya Swift Yasgur, MA, LSW
November 28, 2017

The chronic use of benzodiazepines is
known to increase the death rate of the
mentally ill. See:
Mortality of Patients Dependent on
Benzodiazepines
B Piesiur-Strehlow, U Strehlow, W Poser
Acta Psychiatr Scand 986 Mar;73(3):330-5.
doi: 10.1111/j.1600-0447.1986.tb02693.x.
PMID: 3716850 DOI: 10.1111/j.1600-
0447.1986.tb02693.x

Benzodiazepines increase the death rate
of patients with schizophrenia. See:
Polypharmacy with Antipsychotics,
Antidepressants, or Benzodiazepines and
Mortality in Schizophrenia

Jari Tiihonen, MD, PhD; Jaana T. Suokas, MD, PhD; Jaana M. Suvisaari, MD, PhD; et alJari Haukka, PhD; Pasi Korhonen, PhD
Author Affiliations Article Information
Arch Gen Psychiatry. 2012;69(5):476-483.
doi:10.1001/archgenpsychiatry.2011.1532

The use of benzodiazepines and sleeping pills increase mortality by 40% to 60%.
See:
Mortality associated with anxiolytic and hypnotic drugs—A systematic review and meta-analysis
Ajay K Parsaik, Soniya S Mascarenhas, Darrow Khosh-Chashm, ...
First Published November 20, 2015
Review Article Find in PubMed
https://doi.org/10.1177/0004867415616695

The mentally retarded and the developmentally disabled are not competent to accept the risks and benefits.

The mentally retarded and the developmentally disabled are not able to give informed consent.

Read the following to articles for a detailed explanation.

■■■■■■■■■■■■■■■■■■■■■■■■■■■■■■■■■■■■■■■■■■■■ⁱ

Why I Don't Prescribe Benzodiazepines
William R. Yee M.D., J.D.
Copyright applied for June 28th, 2020

The long-term use of benzodiazepines and sleeping pills such as Ambien is a gold mine waiting to be exploited by plaintiff attorneys.

Review the Johnson and Johnson and Janssen Pharmaceutical Company $572 million dollar judgment to understand the nature and extent of the risk. Then ask your malpractice insurance what the risk is for you. Your insurance may in fact require you to notify them of the risk in order for them to defend a lawsuit. Consult with a California Attorney because I am licensed to practice law in Michigan, and I do not practice law.

I have been taking my patients off benzodiazepines since 1972.

About forty years ago the Physician's Desk Reference, (PDR), reported that Xanax could cause withdrawal seizures with only an exposure of five days. Rare, but real according to the PDR.

The current best practice with benzodiazepines is not to prescribe them for more than two to four weeks. With Xanax that might be for less than five days.

It is well known that anxiolytics and sedative hypnotics including benzodiazepines and Ambien increase depression and suicide.

It is also known that the anxiolytic effect dissipates with addiction while the increased depression and suicide risk persists with the continued use of anxiolytics and sedative hypnotics.

Since I am accustomed to treating the severely mentally ill with a history of suicidal episodes I do not consider use of anxiolytics and sedative hypnotics as appropriate for the patients I have been treating since 1972.

It is well known that anxiolytics and sedative hypnotics including benzodiazepines and Ambien are contraindicated in patients with a history of drug abuse and dependence.

That is another group of severely mentally ill that I have been treating since 1972.

It has been estimated that 15% of the population take benzodiazepines (BZD) in any given year and that the practice is increasing.

This is in the context of the opioid epidemic driven by the Joint Commission using pain as a fifth vital sign and forcing physicians to attempt to relieve patients of all complaints of pain to the point of prescribing PRN opioids for, "breakthrough," pain.

It is well known that adding benzodiazepines to opioids is a cause of respiratory arrest and death.

I submit that adding Ambien and benzodiazepines to sleep apnea and other medical conditions increases the risk of death.

The literature is that benzodiazepines and sedative hypnotics are contraindicated in the presence of sleep apnea and chronic obstructive pulmonary disease.

The long-term use of antidepressants has been associated with a higher death rate as documented by prior research.

However, I don't recall the citation while writing this article.

The use of benzodiazepines is an off-label use for most mental illnesses that should be discouraged because it is well known that addicting medications are only effective for the short term and after addiction, they are not effective.

In fact, during withdrawals, it is well known that the rebound anxiety, rebound insomnia and rebound pain are worse than the original anxiety, insomnia and pain that existed before the addicting medications were prescribed.

Just look at a patient in delirium tremens or DT's to appreciate the severity of anxiety during withdrawal episodes.

FDA approved medications for PTSD include sertraline and paroxetine which are not addicting.

Clinical practice guidelines do not generally support long term use of benzodiazepines because of the addiction and the rebound anxiety that is worse than the original anxiety.

Long-term use of benzodiazepines includes, but is not limited to, the elderly, panic disorder, agoraphobia, chronic and vague symptoms associated with chronic dysphoria and chronic insomnia, patients with personality disorders, substance use disorders, and borderline personality disorder.

Basically, they are used in patients that are treatment failures with psychotropic medications.

Very often the benzodiazepines are abused by the patient or sold as a secondary source of income. This is called diversion. The literature does not support the above long-term use of benzodiazepines.

There is evidence that the use of benzodiazepines after trauma increases the incidence of PTSD by two to five times the rate of those not treated with benzodiazepines.

The adverse effects of benzodiazepines include anxiety, panic attacks, phobias and social avoidance which results in demands for increase in the benzodiazepines.

The patient often confuses the initial euphoric effects experienced during the short period when the blood levels of benzodiazepines are rising with relief from anxiety.

That is why they demand the medication despite the fact it is making their anxiety transform into panic disorder.

Benzodiazepines are contraindicated in patients with a history of substance abuse, depression, suicidal ideation, bipolar disorder, psychosis, and neurocognitive disorders including those due to TBI and depression.

The elderly are known to suffer from memory impairment, confusion, falls and hip fractures due to the use of benzodiazepines, sleeping pills and sedative hypnotics.

The elderly generally improve in function when taken off benzodiazepines.

Benzodiazepines have a host of adverse effects that mimic ADHD and dementia and explosive personality disorder including but not limited to paradoxical agitation, behavioral dysregulation, disinhibition, irritability, cognitive dysfunction, inattention, impaired cognitive processing, and inability to assess risk, inability to assess trauma, inability to assess stress, amnesia, dissociative states, and loss of the ability to fear dangerous activity.

Benzodiazepines cause paradoxical long-term worsening of anxiety.

Benzodiazepines cause brain damage which is diagnosed as benzodiazepine-induced persisting amnestic disorder.

Benzodiazepines and alcohol are known to worsen sleep and sleep architecture as evidenced by sleep EEG's.

Benzodiazepines are associated with fetal addiction, birth defects and should not be prescribed to breastfeeding mothers.

The following medications have stronger evidence for long term efficacy for anxiety than benzodiazepines:
anticonvulsants
antihistamines
antipsychotics
monoamine oxidase inhibitors
serotonergic medications
SNRIs,
SSRIs
tricyclic medications:
Benadryl Diphenhydramine 25mg to 400mg/day X 1 year
Buspar Buspirone 5mg to 60mg/day X 1 year
Catapres Clonidine 0.1mg to 2.4mg/day X 1 year

Depakote Valproate 125mg to 6000mg/day
X 1 year
Inderal Propranolol 10mg to 640mg/day X
1 year
Lamictal Lamotrigine 25mg to 400mg/day
X 1 year
Liothyronine Triiodothyronine 25 Mgm to
50 Mgm/day X 1 year
Lyrica Pregabalin 25mg to 330mg/day X 1
year
Memantine Donepezil 5mg to 28mg/day X
1 year
Minipres Prazosin 1mg to 40mg/day X 1
year
Neurontin Gabapentin 100mg to
3600mg/day X 1 year
Remeron Mirtazapine 7.5mg to 45mg/day
X 1 year
Risperdal Risperidone 0.25mg to
16mg/day X 1 year
Seroquel Quetiapine 25mg to 750mg/day X
1 year
Tenex Guanfacine 0.5mg to 4.0mg/day X 1
year
Trazodone 50mg to 600mg/day X 1 year
Topamax Topiramate  25mg to 400mg/day
X 1 year
Vistaril Hydroxyzine 50mg to 400mg/day X
1 year

Zyprexa Olanzapine 2.5mg to 30mg/day X 1 year.

In general, the best practice is the lowest effective dose.

The use of Benzodiazepines should be restricted for a few days in the PHF or psychiatric hospital.

Patients should not be sent home with a prescription for benzodiazepines, sleeping pills and other addicting medications.

If this were the practice, there might be a substantial reduction in the use of the PHF and psychiatric hospitals.

Time will tell that tale.

The Gold Standard for treating anxiety and PTSD is in fact psychotherapy, including but not limited to CBT, exposure and extinction to stressors sometimes called flooding, relaxation and deep breathing, eye movement desensitization and reprocessing.

Serotonergic agents are approved by the FDA for anxiety, panic, and PTSD, but have a very slow onset of effect of six to twelve weeks.

For insomnia the patient should be directed to a sleep clinic for a sleep EEG and comprehensive evaluation and treatment which are beyond the resources of your facility.

In fact, insurance requires referral from the primary physicians and often do not allow the psychiatrist to refer a patient to a sleep clinic for a sleep EEG and comprehensive evaluation and treatment of insomnia.

Many times, patients have asked me for sleeping pills.

When I advised them that they should go to a sleep clinic for a sleep a comprehensive diagnostic evaluation and a sleep EEG, they had already had a sleep EEG, were diagnosed with sleep apnea, given a C-PAP machine, didn't use it because it was uncomfortable, and now they wanted me to prescribe a sleeping pill.

I advised them that a sleeping pill could kill them in their sleep.

I advised them that I was here to do no harm and to help them if I could.

They were still disappointed when I refused to prescribe a sleeping pill.

They did not formally ask for physician assisted suicide which is an option in California.

I suspect that they were either drug addicts or selling the sleeping pills as a source of income.

 Suspicions are not facts.

The truth is an imaginary construct and I doubt if anyone has ever actually encountered it.

The above is based upon my personal experience treating mental illness since 1972 and the following meta-analysis of the literature on the use of long-term benzodiazepines.

Benzodiazepines I: Upping the Care on Downers: The Evidence of Risks, Benefits and Alternatives
Jeffrey Guina, and Brian Merrill
J Clin Med. 2018 Feb; 7(2): 17.
Published online 2018 Jan 30. doi: 10.3390/jcm7020017
PMCID: PMC5852433
PMID: 29385731

I am here to do no harm and to help if I can.

Thank you for your time and attention.

William R. Yee M.D., J.D.,
Board Certified Psychiatrist practicing psychiatry in Michigan, Indiana, Kentucky and California since 1972 without interruption and recently licensed in Texas, at your service.

The preexisting text includes the names of medications, of people, of lawsuits, of companies, and the articles cited, and the content of articles cited.

My claim is to the original text which is my commentary on the preexisting text that includes the names of medications, of people, of lawsuits, of companies, and the articles cited, and the content of articles cited.

**************************

Why I Recommend Conservators for My Mentally Retarded Patients.
William R. Yee M.D., J.D. Copyright applied for 06/13/2020

IQ is measured by formal psychological tests such as the Wechsler Adult Intelligence Scale (WAIS).

People measure IQ informally without awareness anytime they communicate with another person.

They measure it by dress, grooming, hygiene, smell, social skills, speech, behavior, address, car, purse, money, job title, education, family, etc.

Most Americans have an IQ between 80 and 120.

An IQ below eighty results in substantial global impairment in the ability to function independently.

This fact was explored in art by John Steinbeck in his novella, "Of Mice and Men."

This fact was pointed out by Judge Brennen in his dissenting opinion in Penry v. Lynaugh, 492 U.S. 302, 345 and quoting from the Brief for the AAMR as Amici Curiae at p. 5.

This fact was explored in the context of the death penalty by BEYOND REASON: The Death Penalty and Offenders with Mental Retardation, Human Rights Watch 50 March 2001, Vol. 13,No. 1(G)

An I.Q. below 70 is in the bottom 2 percent of the American population.

An IQ of 60 to 70 is the intellect of an average eight-year old in the third grade.

A third grader cannot buy alcohol, cigarettes or guns. A third grader cannot vote, drive a car, or serve in the military.

A third grader cannot contract to buy a car or a house.

A third grader cannot marry or consent to sex.

A third grader cannot obtain birth control. A third grader cannot consent to a sex change operation or other surgery.

A third grader cannot consent to physician assisted suicide.

I do not believe that a third grader can consent to take medications that can cause death, cause polycystic ovaries, cause liver, failure, cause renal failure, cause sudden death from cardiac arrhythmias, cause a need for tracheotomies and gastrotomies from tardive dyskinesia, and a host of other medical problems.

As a physician I do no harm.

I am my brother's keeper.

If my mentally retarded patients suffer these side effects without the counsel of a conservator or legal guardian, I can be accused of abuse of a dependent adult.

Review the statutes.

That is why I recommend conservators for my mentally retarded patients.

Thank you for your time and attention in these matters.

William R. Yee M.D., J.D.

**The pre-existing text includes the names of people, titles of previously published articles and court cases and the text of the previously published articles and text.**

**My claim is to the original text which is my commentary on the names of people, titles of previously published articles and court cases and the context of the previously published articles and text**

**CHAPTER 13. Crimes Against Elders, Dependent Adults, and Persons with Disabilities [368 - 368.7]**
**(Chapter 13 heading added by Stats. 2010, Ch. 617, Sec. 2.)**

(a) The Legislature finds and declares that elders, adults whose physical or mental disabilities or other limitations restrict their ability to carry out normal activities or to protect their rights, and adults admitted as inpatients to a 24-hour health facility deserve special consideration and protection.

(b) (1) A person who knows or reasonably should know that a person is an elder or dependent adult and who, under circumstances or conditions likely to produce great bodily harm or death, willfully causes or permits any elder or dependent adult to suffer, or inflicts thereon unjustifiable physical pain or mental suffering, or having the care or custody of any elder or dependent adult, willfully causes or permits the person or health of the elder or dependent adult to be injured, or willfully causes or permits the elder or dependent adult to be placed in a situation in which his or her person or health is endangered, is punishable by imprisonment in a county jail not exceeding one year, or by a fine not to exceed six thousand dollars ($6,000), or by both that fine and imprisonment, or by imprisonment in the state prison for two, three, or four years.

(2) If, in the commission of an offense described in paragraph (1), the victim suffers great bodily injury, as defined in Section 12022.7, the defendant shall receive an additional term in the state prison as follows:

(A) Three years if the victim is under 70 years of age.

(B) Five years if the victim is 70 years of age or older.

(3) If, in the commission of an offense described in paragraph (1), the defendant proximately causes the death of the victim, the defendant shall receive an additional term in the state prison as follows:

(A) Five years if the victim is under 70 years of age.

(B) Seven years if the victim is 70 years of age or older.

(c) A person who knows or reasonably should know that a person is an elder or dependent adult and who, under circumstances or conditions other than those likely to produce great bodily harm or death, willfully causes or permits any elder or dependent adult to suffer, or inflicts thereon unjustifiable physical pain or mental suffering, or having the care or custody of any elder or dependent adult, willfully causes or permits the person or health of the elder or dependent adult to be injured or willfully causes or permits the elder or dependent adult to be placed in a situation in which his or her person or health may be endangered, is guilty of a misdemeanor. A second or subsequent violation of this subdivision is punishable by a fine not to exceed two thousand dollars ($2,000), or by imprisonment in a county jail not to exceed one year, or by both that fine and imprisonment.

(d) A person who is not a caretaker who violates any provision of law proscribing theft, embezzlement, forgery, or fraud, or who violates Section 530.5 proscribing identity theft, with respect to the property or personal identifying information of an elder or a dependent adult, and who knows or reasonably should know that the victim is an elder or a dependent adult, is punishable as follows:

(1) By a fine not exceeding two thousand five hundred dollars ($2,500), or by

imprisonment in a county jail not exceeding one year, or by both that fine and imprisonment, or by a fine not exceeding ten thousand dollars ($10,000), or by imprisonment pursuant to subdivision (h) of Section 1170 for two, three, or four years, or by both that fine and imprisonment, when the moneys, labor, goods, services, or real or personal property taken or obtained is of a value exceeding nine hundred fifty dollars ($950).

(2) By a fine not exceeding one thousand dollars ($1,000), by imprisonment in a county jail not exceeding one year, or by both that fine and imprisonment, when the moneys, labor, goods, services, or real or personal property taken or obtained is of a value not exceeding nine hundred fifty dollars ($950).

(e) A caretaker of an elder or a dependent adult who violates any provision of law proscribing theft, embezzlement, forgery, or fraud, or who violates Section 530.5 proscribing identity theft, with respect to the property or personal identifying information of that elder or dependent adult, is punishable as follows:

(1) By a fine not exceeding two thousand five hundred dollars ($2,500), or by imprisonment in a county jail not exceeding one year, or by both that fine and imprisonment, or by a fine not exceeding ten thousand dollars ($10,000), or by imprisonment pursuant to subdivision (h) of Section 1170 for two, three, or four years, or by both that fine and imprisonment, when the moneys, labor, goods, services, or real or personal property taken or obtained is of a value exceeding nine hundred fifty dollars ($950).

(2) By a fine not exceeding one thousand dollars ($1,000), by imprisonment in a county jail not exceeding one year, or by both that fine and imprisonment, when the moneys, labor, goods, services, or real or personal property taken or obtained is of a value not exceeding nine hundred fifty dollars ($950).

(f) A person who commits the false imprisonment of an elder or a dependent adult by the use of violence, menace, fraud, or deceit is punishable by imprisonment pursuant to subdivision (h) of Section 1170 for two, three, or four years.

(g) As used in this section, "elder" means a person who is 65 years of age or older.

(h) As used in this section, "dependent adult" means a person, regardless of whether the person lives independently, who is between the ages of 18 and 64, who has physical or mental limitations which restrict his or her ability to carry out normal activities or to protect his or her rights, including, but not limited to, persons who have physical or developmental disabilities or whose physical or mental abilities have diminished because of age. "Dependent adult" includes a person between the ages of 18 and 64 who is admitted as an inpatient to a 24-hour health facility, as defined in Sections 1250, 1250.2, and 1250.3 of the Health and Safety Code.

(i) As used in this section, "caretaker" means a person who has the care, custody, or control of, or who stands in a position of trust with, an elder or a dependent adult.

(j) Nothing in this section shall preclude prosecution under both this section and Section 187 or 12022.7 or any other provision of law. However, a person shall not receive an additional term of imprisonment under both paragraphs (2) and (3) of subdivision (b) for a single offense, nor shall a person receive an additional term of imprisonment under both Section 12022.7 and paragraph (2) or (3) of subdivision (b) for a single offense.

(k) In any case in which a person is convicted of violating these provisions, the court may require him or her to receive appropriate counseling as a condition of probation. A defendant ordered to be placed in a counseling program shall be responsible for paying the expense of his or her participation in the counseling program as determined by the court. The court shall take into consideration the ability of the defendant to pay, and no defendant shall be denied probation because of his or her inability to pay.

(l) Upon conviction for a violation of subdivision (b), (c), (d), (e), or (f), the sentencing court shall also consider issuing an order restraining the defendant from any contact with the victim, which may be valid for up to 10 years, as determined by the court. It is the intent of the Legislature that the length of any restraining order be based upon the

seriousness of the facts before the court, the probability of future violations, and the safety of the victim and his or her immediate family. This protective order may be issued by the court whether the defendant is sentenced to state prison or county jail, or if imposition of sentence is suspended and the defendant is placed on probation.
(Amended by Stats. 2018, Ch. 70, Sec. 3. (AB 1934) Effective January 1, 2019.)

"Preexisting text," includes names of symptoms, medical illnesses, medications, people, corporations, law cases, statues, text of statutes, the titles of articles, of books, the content of articles and books cited.

My copyright claim is a clam to the "original text," which is my personal experiences as described in the text above and my commentary on the names of symptoms, medical illnesses, medications, people, corporations, law cases, statues, text of statutes, the titles of articles, of books, the content of articles and books cited.

High Dose Antipsychotics and Polypharmacy

There is no persuasive evidence that high doses of antipsychotic medications or polypharmacy are more effective than low dos antipsychotic medications.

See:
Reducing the rates of prescribing high-dose antipsychotics and polypharmacy on psychiatric inpatient and intensive care units: results of a 6-year quality improvement programme
Shubhra Mace, David Taylor
First Published November 9, 2014
Research Article Find in PubMed
https://doi.org/10.1177/2045125314558054

There is no high dose of antipsychotic medication or polypharrnacy that is more effective than low dose antipsychotic medications.

See:
Reducing the rates of prescribing high-dose antipsychotics and polypharmacy on psychiatric inpatient and intensive care

units: results of a 6-year quality
improvement programme
Shubhra Mace, David Taylor
First Published November 9, 2014
Research Article Find in PubMed
https://doi.org/10.1177/2045125314558054

No pharmacological combination
treatment is superior to antipsychotic
monotherapy.

No pharmacologic combination treatment
can be recommended for the treatment of
schizophrenia.

See:
Efficacy of 42 Pharmacologic Cotreatment
Strategies Added to Antipsychotic
Monotherapy in SchizophreniaSystematic
Overview and Quality Appraisal of the
Meta-analytic Evidence
Christoph U. Correll, MD1,2,3; Jose M.
Rubio, MD1; Gabriella Inczedy-Farkas,
MD1; et alMichael L. Birnbaum, MD1,2,3;
John M. Kane, MD1,2,3; Stefan Leucht,
MD4
Author Affiliations Article Information
JAMA Psychiatry. 2017;74(7):675-684.
doi:10.1001/jamapsychiatry.2017.0624

Adverse effects of high dose antipsychotic medication are serious and numerous.

Polypharmacy increases adverse effects.

The longer the treatment the greater the severity of medication side effects.

Clozapine has worse side effects than other antipsychotic medications.

Hyperprolactinemia occurs more often in women than in men.

There is a low baseline monitoring of lipids and glucose.

Management of adverse effects are not adequately developed.

See:
"First do no harm." A systematic review of the prevalence and management of antipsychotic adverse effects
Su Ling Young, Mark Taylor, Stephen M Lawrie
First Published December 16, 2014 Review Article Find in PubMed

https://doi.org/10.1177/0269881114562090

\*\*\*\*\*\*\*\*\*\*\*\*\*\*\*\*\*\*\*\*\*\*\*\*\*\*\*\*\*\*\*

Why the Lowest Effective Dose is the Best Practice?
Because there is a limit to physiologic reserve.
William R. Yee M.D., J.D. Board Certified Psychiatrist.

Physiologic Reserve is a measure of the body's ability to survive any imaginable stress such as heat, cold, poison, COVID-19, head injuries, and starvation,

An important example is the stress of seizure medications on the pregnant woman and her fetus.

Monotherapy is preferable to polytherapy with AEDs because the risk of major malformations is as high as one in four, or 25%, in infants of women who are taking 4 or more AEDs.
See:
Antiepileptic drugs during pregnancy: What is

known and which AEDs seem to be safest?
Page B. Pennell Epilepsia. 2008 Dec;
49(0  9):   10.1111/j.1528-1167.2008.01926.x.
doi: 10.1111/j.1528-1167.2008.01926.x;
PMCID:        PMC3882069;        NIHMSID:
NIHMS531069; PMID: 19087117

The risk of death from COVOD-19 is increased with age, obesity, diabetes, and high blood pressure.

It is important to encourage weight loss and aerobic exercise to reduce diabetes, reduce hypertension and increase physiologic reserve thereby reducing the risk of death with COVOD-19 and other stressors.

The risk of Tardive Dyskinesia is increased by increasing the lifetime exposure to metoclopramide, amitriptyline, fluoxetine, phenelzine, sertraline, trazodone, levodopa, phenobarbital, phenytoin, haloperidol, chlorpromazine and most of the antipsychotic medications.

It is therefore important to limit the lifetime exposure to medications by offering CBT, EMDR, meditation, aerobic exercise, sleep hygiene, individual and group therapies, and any other available alternative to medications when treating mental illness.

That is why I advise the patient that they should consider medication tapers when symptoms are controlled to identify the lowest effective dose of medications. Very often, the lowest effective dose is no medication at all.

That is why the lowest effective dose is the best practice in medicine.

Thank you for your time and attention. William R. Yee M.D., J.D. Board Certified Psychiatrist

The preexisting text includes the names of people, treatment modalities, and medications, the titles and content of articles mentioned.

The original text claimed is my commentary on the preexisting text including medications, people, treatment modalities, the articles and content of articles cited above.

Why I Practice Medicine the Way I Do
I Have No Choice
Except to Help When I Can
Your 13th Psychiatric Consultation
William Yee M.D., J.D.
Copyright Applied for 06/30/2020

I do what I am compelled to do when I am practicing medicine.
First, I do no harm.

Second, I help when I can. This is the only thing I want to do.

Third, it is always the patient's choice, not my choice.

Fourth, it is always the best practice.

The best practice is the practic with the least risk.

Meditation carries the least risk and costs little.

Aerobic exercise carries little risk and little expense.

Psychotherapy is safer than psychotropic medications.

The lowest effective dose is safer that any higher dose of medication.

Short periods of medications are safer than longer periods of medication exposures.

Single medications are safer and cheaper than combinations of medications.

The criteria for admission to a psychiatric hospital is suicidal, homicidal, or so gravely disabled that a patient cannot be safely or effectively treated outside of a hospital.

Outpatient treatment is safer than hospital treatment because staff and patients are assaulted, injured and occasionally killed in psychiatric hospitals.

I help when I can.

Other than helping, I never do what I want to do while practicing medicine.

\*\*\*\*\*\*\*\*\*\*\*\*\*\*\*\*\*\*\*\*\*\*\*\*\*\*

In summary, it is advisable to use single antipsychotics at low doses for schizophrenia.

For bipolar disorder and schizoaffective disorder it may be necessary to combine a mood stabilizer with an antidepressant or an antipsychotic.

In all cases medication tapers need to be offered, and that offer needs to be documented.

Thank you for your time and attention. William R. Yee M.D., J.D.

"Preexisting text," includes names of symptoms, medical illnesses, medications, people, corporations, law cases, statues, text of statutes, the titles of articles, of books, the content of articles and books cited.

My copyright claim is a clam to the "original text," which is my personal experiences as described in the text above and my commentary on the names of symptoms, medical illnesses, medications, people, corporations, law cases, statues, text of statutes, the titles of articles, of books, the content of articles and books cited.